Dartmoor
with your Kids

Robert Hesketh

with thanks to Verity, Tamsin and Adrienne

Bossiney Books · Launceston

First published 2006 by
Bossiney Books Ltd, Langore, Launceston, Cornwall PL15 8LD
www.bossineybooks.com

ISBN 0-1-899383-86-7
ISBN 978-189938386-3

Acknowledgements
The map is by Graham Hallowell
Photographs by the author
except that on page 13 which is from the publishers' own collection
Printed in Great Britain by St Austell Printing Company Ltd

Introduction

The pleasant dilemma faced by parents is not so much what to do with their kids on Dartmoor, but how to find the time to cover the many, many possibilities in southern England's largest (and highest) wilderness. Some of the best activities for children are free or inexpensive. I've aimed to give a good range of suggestions to suit children of all ages and various interests. I make no apologies if some seem simple or even old-fashioned – kids can play happily and creatively without play stations and theme parks.

Please note that this book is a general guide rather than an annual publication. Changes are bound to occur from one year to the next. Entrance fees, where applicable, are indicated in general terms only.

No publication of this size can cover everything, but it can be the key, the starting point, to a wealth of interesting and constructive activities, which will keep your kids happy and occupied. That sounds like a recipe for a good holiday to me...

An Ordnance Survey Explorer map OL 28 and a copy of *Dartmoor Visitor* (free from local information centres) will help enormously.

Please remember to follow the Country Code and be careful not to feed the ponies (they become vulnerable to traffic accidents if lured to the roads by food) or disturb birds during the nesting season.

Information and enquiries

The following list covers the main sources of information for visitors to Dartmoor.

Dartmoor National Park Authority (DNPA)
(01626 832093 www.dartmoor-npa.gov.uk)
Offers information on weather, public transport, live firing on ranges, Dartmoor factsheets and leaflets, guided walks and events (events hotline 01822 890414). Teachers and group leaders can contact the Education Service on 01626 831080.

DNPA Information Centres offer a variety of local information and literature, including walks leaflets. Ask for a copy of the *Dartmoor Visitor* – it is issued by the DNPA, is free, and has a lot of useful information, including a timetable of guided walks and events.

Lustleigh May Day celebrations

The DNPA Information Centres
High Moorland Visitor Centre, Princetown 01822 890414
Newbridge 01364 631303
Postbridge 01822 880272
Haytor 01364 661520

Tourist Information Centres (TICs)
Ashburton 01364 653426
Bovey Tracey 01626 832047
Moretonhampstead 01647 440043
Okehampton 01837 53020
Tavistock 01822 612938

Other visitor centres considerably further afield in Devon, in particular those at Crediton, Dartmouth, Plymouth and Totnes, also have a great deal of information about Dartmoor.

Live firing on ranges
There are three military ranges (marked on the Ordnance Survey map) on the remotest parts of Northern Dartmoor, marked on the

ground by red and white posts, with warning notices. Check firing times before you enter these areas by contacting:

0800 458 4868, www.dartmoor-ranges.co.uk *or*
DNPA 01626 832093, www.dartmoor-npa.gov.uk.

Leave alone any strange objects you find in case they are unexploded shells, and contact the police with a map reference.

Public transport

For timetable information on all services: 0870 608 2608
DNPA: 01626 832093 (www.dartmoor-npa.gov.uk)
Devon Bus Enquiry Line: 01392 382800 devonbus@devon.gov.uk

Local events

Dartmoor is rich in local traditions and annual celebrations. The TICs and the magazine *Dartmoor Visitor* will have details. Kids will particularly enjoy *Lustleigh's May Day*, when the May Queen is crowned and there is a procession with maypole dancing and live music in the Orchard.

Another favourite is *Widecombe Fair* in September, with ponies, stalls, a race, entertainments and Uncle Tom Cobley.

Less well-known is Ashburton's *Ale Tasting and Bread Weighing* ceremony in July. The town's officials process through the town in medieval costume, calling at all the inns and bakeries. Street entertainments include Morris dancing and a bread auction.

In August, the annual *Dartmoor Folk Festival* is held at South Zeal, near Okehampton. It follows on from the Sidmouth Folk Festival, but is a much smaller and very friendly affair. Musicians, dancers and entertainers from all over the county and some from further afield delight people of all ages for a modest admission charge. There are special acts for children, plus dance classes and opportunities to join the singing. Weather permitting, many of the events take place outdoors, but there are marquees too, whilst some events are held in local pubs. The craft stalls are particularly interesting.

Carnivals, fetes and fairs are held around Dartmoor, mainly in the summer. Bovey Tracey's *Carnival* and its *Vintage Vehicle Rally* are especially good. Tavistock *Goose Fair* is in October and there are various fairs and street markets before Christmas, such as those at Tavistock, Okehampton, Lustleigh and Bovey Tracey, where people often dress in period costume.

Altogether, local events are a great way to see Dartmoor life and meet local people. Visitors – especially with children – are welcome. In fact, the long term future of local events (and much else on Dartmoor) depends on visitor support.

Activities

Dartmoor National Park organised activities

Cost: admission charge for children; accompanying adults free
Contact: 01626 832093; see also *Dartmoor Visitor* for programme
Weather: outdoor activities; please bring suitable clothing

Like the Devon Wildlife Trust (page 18), Dartmoor National Park runs a variety of interesting, constructive and well-organised activities for children, such as stream dipping, discovery trails, walks, nestbox building and navigation. These are a great introduction to Dartmoor and its wildlife. The DNPA programme also includes guided walks and local events (page 10).

'Ranger Ralph' is a club designed mainly for 8-12 year olds to have fun on Dartmoor. Members receive various gifts and a newsletter detailing events such as den building and willow weaving. Ralph's walks and cycle rides come with cartoons and quizzes. Also recommended is Ralph the Ranger's *Children's Guide to Dartmoor*, a well-designed and child friendly production, available from DNPA centres.

Seasonal interest

Whilst many of the activities in this book can be enjoyed all the year round or for a good part of the year, some belong to particular seasons or months. This is a short list of interesting things to do and look out for month by month. You could award your kids stars or treats for spotting the first snowdrop, Dartmoor pony foal or running salmon. Some highlights, such as lambing and the dawn chorus, spread over several months.

    January: snowdrops, new lambs
    February: frog spawn, first primroses
    March: wild daffodils (try the B3212 Teign Valley road and Steps Bridge)
    April: return of the summer birds, especially martins, swifts and swallows

April through July: Peregrine Watch (page 19)

May: new Dartmoor pony foals, Lustleigh May Day

June: dawn chorus

July: Ashburton Ale Tasting

August: heather in flower, Dartmoor Folk Festival, whortleberries

September: Widecombe Fair, blackberries, swaling (controlled burning of old heather and gorse – please do not attempt it!)

October: autumn colours

November: sea trout and salmon running (try the Teign between Castle Drogo and Dogmarsh Bridge at SX 893714)

December: first new lambs on moorland edges, local craft fairs, churches decorated for Christmas

Storytelling

Bored and fractious kids can be turned into interested and lively ones with a good story. Some like to draw pictures around stories or invent games. Older children may prefer to do the story-telling.

Dartmoor has some great stories of its own, with dramatic settings to fire young imaginations… and get children walking. Some are shown with impressive and really scary photographs at the High Moorland Visitor Centre, Princetown.

Arthur Conan Doyle's *Hound of the Baskervilles* is the best known Dartmoor story, partly inspired by local legends. Raise the hair on the back of their necks with 'Grimpen Mire' (based on Fox Tor Mire, 5 km south of Princetown at SX 626703), where the villain dies a terrible death by drowning, but remember the mire is best seen from the edge because it really is boggy and can be dangerous.

Conjure the frightening and deadly hound with his glowing eyes among the fantastic rock piles at Hound Tor near Manaton. Hound Tor is also said to be the pack of hounds turned to stone when their master, Bowerman, was punished for taking them hunting over the moor on a Sunday. Bowerman himself broods over the scene nearby at Bowerman's Nose (SX 743805), a granite pile that certainly looks like a face.

Vixen Tor (SX 543743) near Merrivale is said to have been the home of an evil witch, Vixana. She called down those notorious Dartmoor mists to lure travellers to their deaths in a nearby mire. One day a young man came to Vixana. She did not know that this man too had magic powers. He could see through mists and make himself invisible. As Vixana stood on her tor, waiting for the cold mist to clear, he crept up behind her and gave her a sudden push…

Crockern Tor (SX 616757) near Two Bridges, where the traditional Stannary of Tinners' Parliament is still held, is haunted by Old Crockern, a moorland spirit. On stormy nights he and his skeleton horse are sometimes seen or heard clattering over the rocks.

Possibly, this story is related to that of Childe's Tomb, an impressive structure at a lonely spot on the edge of Fox Tor Mire. Centuries ago, Childe the Hunter was caught in a terrible snow storm here. His horse seemed to offer his only chance of survival, so he killed the beast and sheltered in its belly. Sadly, he froze to death anyway.

The Moretonhampstead to Princetown road is said to be haunted between Postbridge and Two Bridges. Several motorcyclists have been killed on this stretch – their machines wrenched from their control by a mysterious pair of huge and hairy hands… just like Daddy's!

Lightning struck Widecombe's church tower in 1638. It collapsed into the congregation and killed four people. Naturally, tales soon sprang up that the Devil was behind this terrible event. He is said to have visited various local spots en route to Widecombe, including the Tavistock Inn at Poundsgate, where he left scorch marks on the bar and paid his bill with withered leaves.

Swimming

Swimming is not especially a Dartmoor activity, but a longish drive to the coast can be avoided by using local public swimming pools. There are outdoor pools, usually open only during the summer, at:

Ashburton (01364 6528280)
Bovey Tracey (01626 832828)
Chagford (01647 43343)
Moretonhampstead (01647 440134)

and indoor pools at:

Ivybridge (01752 896999)
Newton Abbot (01626 215640)
Okehampton (01837 659154)
Tavistock (01822 617774)

Cycling

Contact 0870 608 5531 (www.devon-online.com/dartmoor-cycling *or* www.discoverdevon.com) for a brochure of cycling trails in Devon. Dartmoor National Park publish a route map of mountain bike routes.

Cycle hire:

   Dartmoor Cycles, Tavistock (01822 618178)
   Moor Cycles, Okehampton (01837 659677)
   Mountain Bike Centre, Ashburton
     (01364 654080 www.big-peaks.com)
   Okehampton Cycles (01837 53248)
   Tavistock Cycles (01822 617630)

Dartmoor offers a variety of enjoyable cycling. There are two fairly gentle-surfaced cycle routes and some challenging off-road routes too, some with tough gradients. Contact DNPA.

A network of beautiful but narrow lanes links Dartmoor's villages. Cycling them gives a real sense of discovery. These lanes are mainly on the eastern edge of the moor and usually hilly, often with high hedge-banks, thick with wildflowers in spring. Altogether, they are a delight to explore if you and your kids are fit and experienced cyclists and are used to reading maps.

If you're new to cycling, the Meldon and Plym Valley cycle routes offer the best and safest starting points, without compromising scenic pleasure. The *Plym Valley Cycleway* is 11km (7 miles) long, almost level (bar one short section) and traffic free apart from a mile around Bickleigh. Starting by Coypool car park just east of Plymouth, it follows a series of tram and railway beds over marvellous aqueducts to Clearbrook on the edge of Dartmoor, where there is a welcome inn, the Skylark. There is much of interest en route, including industrial archaeology and nesting peregrines, best viewed during the nesting season through the telescopes provided (page 19).

Starting at Okehampton, the *Granite Way* offers superb Dartmoor views on the way to Lydford. With Okehampton Castle (page 26), Lydford Gorge (page 25), the Museum of Dartmoor Life (page 23), plus Okehampton Station, Meldon Visitor Centre and Lydford Castle, there is plenty of interest to make this a good day out. Altogether, the Granite Way is 18km (11 miles) and mainly level. 13.5km (8 1/2 miles) of it are traffic free, the rest on lanes, but with a main road crossing.

Walking

Cost: free except for the equipment. DNPA charge a fee for their guided walks – but there's no charge if you have used public transport to get to the start

Equipment needed: see below

Walking is deservedly the most popular way to explore Dartmoor. It opens up the moor to a far greater extent than a car. Indeed, much of Dartmoor, including most of the prehistoric sites (see page 26-8), is *only* accessible on foot or on horseback.

Kids unused to walking may take some time to get accustomed to it, so it's best to keep the walks short with plenty of interest and include some treats to keep them going. Guided walks are a great way to start. DNPA offers a programme of over 400 walks per year. The shorter walks take under two hours, the longest up to six.

The alternative is to buy the OS Explorer map and a compass, and do your own thing. A book of short walks could be useful – hopefully its author will have identified any problems and avoided them.

Walking on Dartmoor is safe and trouble free – if you are prepared. In the first place, the weather can change suddenly. Please do not go without good walking boots and suitable clothing. Drinking water, plus waterproofs and an extra layer are equally essential, likewise a comfortable rucksack. Many, including me, add a walking stick, mobile phone and food.

In addition to the 723 km (449 miles) of public rights of way, large areas of the moor offer open access, which means you do not have to stick to paths and tracks. Rights of way and open access are shown on the OS Dartmoor Explorer map. For more information and details of guided walks and army firing times contact DNPA (see page 3).

Letterboxing

Equipment needed: an ink pad, a plain book or card for the stamps, an OS Explorer map and a compass Optional extra: your own rubber stamp

Contact: www.letterboxingondartmoor.co.uk;
Tony Moore, Letterbox 100 Club: 100club@bigfoot.com

If your kids like treasure hunts and the outdoors, then they'll enjoy letterboxing, but you'll need at least basic map reading and orienteering skills. If you have a GPS (global positioning system) this would be a considerable bonus. There is a letterbox hidden on most Dartmoor tors and in many places besides. Altogether, there are over 3000 letterboxes, equipped with their own rubber stamps. Collecting the stamps is an added motivation – and can become an obsession!

Each letterbox is a small pot, equipped with a rubber stamp, a visitors' book and a clue to other hiding places. Some clues are simply map references and compass bearings, though others are more cryptic. When you find a letterbox, take a print of the stamp with your ink pad and, if you have your own personal stamp, put a print of it in the visitors' book before re-hiding the pot. People have great fun making their own stamps, but specialist companies also produce them to order. The catalogue available through the website will enable you to find your first letterbox.

Letterboxing began in 1854 when Dartmoor guide James Perrot left the first letterbox at Cranmere Pool. It has gone from strength to strength, spreading around the UK and world-wide.

Please follow the letterboxers' code for finding and siting letterboxes. Essentially, this means respecting Dartmoor's wildlife and its farm animals. Details are given on the website. Also, check that the area is not being used for live firing (page 4).

Pony trekking and hacking

Cost: variable, with hourly, half day and full day rates

Suitable for: anyone who can sit straight on a pony/horse

General information: www.devonponies.co.uk

Sample contacts:

Skaigh Stables (01837 840429, www.skaighstables.co.uk)

Shilstone Rock Stud and Trekking Centre, Widecombe
   (01364 621281)

Lydford House Riding Stables, Lydford (01822 820347,
   perfectridingholidays@lydfordhouse.co.uk)

Fitzworthy Riding, Cornwood (01752 837836)

Eastlake Farm Riding Stables, Belstone (01837 52513)

The open spaces of Dartmoor are ideal for riding and there are a number of stables to choose from. Pony trekking is best for beginners. It's like a gentle guided tour on horseback and is a great way to enjoy the scenery – ponies and riders move in a sedate convoy across the countryside. An hour or two is probably the best way to start trekking for bottoms unaccustomed to the saddle, but half and full day treks are also available for more experienced riders.

Shop around for prices, check that all the tack you need is provided, be honest about your own and your kids' riding experience (or lack of it!) and book in advance – especially during July and August. If your kid is an experienced rider, an exhilarating hack over the wilder parts of the moor is another option, but don't underestimate the unevenness or steepness of the terrain and the changeable nature of Dartmoor weather.

Pond and river dipping

Suggested locations: Dartmeet (SX672732), Belstone Cleave
   (SX622936), Cadover Bridge (SX555646), New Bridge (SX712719)

Precautions: do not attempt after heavy rain – Dartmoor rivers rise
   very suddenly. Keep children supervised at all times – beware of
   deeper and faster water and the very slippery river bed

Remember: towels, old rubber soled shoes with good grips and a
   change of clothing

Equipment: net with long handle; jam jars for temporary storage

Any child who enjoys rockpooling will enjoy its freshwater equivalent

A school party pond dipping at Hay Tor

and Dartmoor has delightful rivers to explore. Ensuring river dipping and paddling are safe is a matter of following the same precautions as by the sea. Children gain great pleasure collecting specimens such as dragonflies, water beetles and pond skaters. Trout fry are extremely quick and virtually uncatchable, but fascinating to watch, once you've learned to distinguish them from their background.

Please encourage your kids to treat all the flora and fauna with respect and return all creatures unharmed to the river. Forbid dam building, which is harmful. Wildlife Action Zones are designed to protect salmon and trout spawning grounds, which can be easily damaged by paddling because the fish lay their eggs in the gravel beds. Please avoid paddling at Pizwell (SX669776), Runnage (SX668788), Lower Cherrybrook (SX632747) and Bellever (SX658773).

Picnics

Dartmoor is ideal for picnics, which combine readily with many other activities for kids such as kite flying, paddling, ball games, painting, collecting art objects and blackberry picking. Below are a few pleasant picnic sites with picnic tables and car parks (marked on OS maps). All have extra points of interest. Please remember NOT to feed the ponies (because human contact reduces their fear of the roads) and to take litter home.

Fernworthy Reservoir, 6km (4 miles) SW of Chagford, SX667837.
   Bird reserve and hide, plus brown trout fishing. Delightful walk around the perimeter of the reservoir.

Postbridge, Moretonhampstead to Princetown road, SX647788.
   Information centre, toilets. One of Dartmoor's best medieval clapper bridges.

Bellever, 2km (1½ miles) S of Postbridge (see above), SX656772.
   Clapper bridge. (Please note this is a Wildlife Action Zone and avoid paddling in the river – it discourages fish from spawning.)

Meldon Reservoir, 6km (4 miles) SW of Okehampton, SX562917.
   Dartmoor Railway nearby. Fishing. Walks. Toilets.

Trenchford Reservoir, 5km (3 miles) N Bovey Tracey, SX805824.
   Toilets, woodland walks, trout fishing at nearby Kennick.

Picnics, one of Dartmoor's simple pleasures – even if you do sometimes need to take an extra layer of clothing!

Pooh sticks

Readers of AA Milne's stories will remember the fun Christopher Robin, Winnie the Pooh and friends had with this simplest of games. Contestants stand on a bridge equipped with sticks. At the word of command from Christopher Robin (or whoever is in charge) they drop their sticks into the river on the upstream side, nip round to the downstream side and see whose stick has won the race. Please ensure children do not damage trees or block streams.

Readers may be interested to know that a certain Mr C R Milne for many years ran the Harbour Bookshop, Dartmouth. He declined – sadly but understandably – to stock the Winnie-the-Pooh titles.

Games kit

'Games kit' may conjure memories of rugby shirts in clashing colours and odoriferous gym shoes, but I just mean a soft ball, a Frisbee, a kite and a colouring book to keep in the boot of the car and produce at picnics, playparks, etc. Your children will, perhaps, have their own favourites to add.

As Dartmoor is a place of open spaces, a simple games kit is always useful. It often gives more fun than expensive and elaborate games and stops kids getting bored at slack moments.

Fishing

Cost: appropriate Environment Agency rod licence (available from some post offices), plus permit needed

Contacts: Environment Agency (08708 506506); Duchy of Cornwall (01822 890205); River Dart (01803 762274); SW Lakes Trust (01566 771930, www.swlakestrust.org.uk); Week Farm, Bridestowe (coarse) (01837 861221 www.weekfarmonline.com/fishing)

Weather: one of the key factors!

Fishing is suitable for older children, and Dartmoor is primarily a game fishing area. If you've mastered fly fishing, the rivers offer good sport, for brown trout, peel (sea trout) and salmon. Much of the water is available to the public, with day, week or season permits available on the River Dart and from the Duchy of Cornwall.

The reservoirs can be a delight too. Kennick near Moretonhampstead is stocked with rainbow trout and offers fair value for an adult full day ticket (substantially cheaper for children). Fly fishing for brown trout at Fernworthy near Chagford and Burrator near Yelverton is also good value.

There is free wilderness trout fishing at Avon Dam near South Brent, at Meldon near Okehampton and at Venford. On these waters fly fishing is allowed, as well as spinning and bait fishing.

If you're new to fly fishing, try Tavistock Trout Fishery (01822 615441), which offers tuition, or Roddy Rae's Fly Fishing School (01626 866532). It takes time and patience to learn casting and enough knowledge to catch fish, but most people (including me!) find fly fishing totally absorbing.

Don't forget your Environment Agency rod licence!

Painting and sketching

When adults claim they cannot draw or paint, they usually mean they haven't tried since they were kids and are embarrassed at their under-developed skills. Small children by contrast love art and get better at it with practice because they are quite uninhibited.

Keep the sketch book and crayons handy – Dartmoor abounds in subjects. Some people like to make quick sketches or take photos and work them into paintings later when they get home, but kids usually like instant results, so you may want to take paints with you.

A simple tool kit – box of paints, pencils from 2H to 4B, crayons, brushes, jam jars, a bottle of water and rags – can easily be kept in the car. You may find, as I did, that your kids enjoy sketching and painting so much you want to have a go too – anyway, they'll probably nag you to show them how to do it!

Craftwork from stray finds

It is amazing what you can find. I recently discovered a hand-made brass car horn in perfect working order beside a Dartmoor river, but what can you do with all those little treasures kids pick up in the countryside – feathers, nuts, pine cones, quartz crystals, pebbles, leaves, horse shoes…?

One solution is to make designs with them. You can simply do this on the ground. That means leaving your design behind, but you can take a photograph.

Alternatively, take some materials home for a collage. Get the kids to lay the design out before glueing anything to your backing – you can use paper, but card, especially coloured card, is better. Wood or metal can also be used for backing – try decorating boxes, mirror frames, etc with found objects.

An extra dimension can be added with paint and brushes. For example, you could paint a background of trees and then make it three dimensional with leaves and nuts. Materials such as stone and wood take oil-based paints well. Hand-painted doorstops and paper weights made of pebbles offer plenty of scope. You've probably seen them in gift shops, but making your own is simple. A spray paint or varnish may give the finish you want, but small children and spray cans do not mix well!

A word of warning – unidentified objects on the north Dartmoor ranges must be left well alone, in case they are unexploded ordnance. Make a note of where you found them and tell the police or the army.

Kite flying

The open windswept moors are perfect for flying a kite, which can be part of your games kit (page 15) and really ought to be part of every-one's childhood. Wind and weather are the key things. Check the fore-cast before going – some wind is obviously needed, preferably a steady breeze that doesn't suddenly drop and leave your kite earthbound.

A bit of drizzle is OK, but heavy rain means a sodden, heavy kite

A Devon Wildlife Trust wildlife walk

and wet, disgruntled kids. Very strong winds must be avoided, especially if only a small kid is attached to the kite!

Benjamin Franklin achieved spectacular results from flying his kite in a thunderstorm. Some say this is how Franklin got his nickname of Old Lightning Rod, others that it referred to his exploits with the fair sex, but this practice – I mean flying kites in a thunderstorm – is really dangerous and should be avoided completely.

Devon Wildlife Trust (DWT)

Cost: modest fee for each child
Contacts: DWT (01392 279244)
 Local Wildlife Watch groups: Clare Davies – 01626 352731 (Bovey/Stover), Jo Pullin – 01392 279244 (Roadford), Fran Rickwood – 01837 659533 (Okehampton), Sue Searle (over 12s Teen Leader) – 01392 209314 (www.devonwildlifetrust.org)
Weather: some indoor activities, some weather dependent – take suitable clothing

Devon Wildlife Trust's junior branch, Wildlife Watch, offers an interesting and varied programme of constructive and well-organised activities throughout the year. Everyone is welcome and Wildlife Watch is an excellent way to find out more about wildlife and meet new friends. There is pond dipping, bird watching, badger spotting, mini beast hunting, plus arts and crafts with a wildlife/conservation flavour and more besides. Over 12s have their own group, based in Exeter.

Much of the adult programme, such as nest box building, slide shows, practical conservation, fungus forays and guided walks, will also appeal to older children.

Altogether, Wildlife Watch gives kids and their parents a fresh perspective on Dartmoor and a super introduction to environmentally friendly activities. (Other counties have similar groups.)

As well as Wildlife Watch, Devon Wildlife Trust has 40 nature reserves to visit around the county. Covering 3300 acres, they offer good access via footpaths (in some cases suitable for disabled visitors – see the website) and helpful display boards. On Dartmoor, the largest is the Dart Valley reserve. A mix of upland moor and unspoilt woodland valley, it is rich in bird and insect life, as well as wild flowers. The best access is from the New Bridge (SX711709) or Dartmeet (SX673733) car parks on the Ashburton to Two Bridges road.

Dunsford Reserve at Steps Bridge (SX803884) on the Exeter to Moretonhampstead road is noted for its wild daffodils and riverside paths. Yarner Wood (SX786788) between Bovey Tracey and Haytor is a haven for woodland birds, as is Lady's Wood near South Brent at SX668951. There is also Bovey Heathfield, a fine example of England's rapidly vanishing lowland heath, which the Trust acquired in 2002 and is restoring after years of abuse. (Access is via the industrial estate at Cavalier Way, SX826763.) Also near Bovey Tracey are Bradley Ponds (SX830778), a home to water-loving birds.

Peregrine watch

Cost: free

Location: Plym Valley Trail, 2km (1¹/₂ miles) N of Plym Bridge at
  SX524596

Parking: free at Plym Bridge SX526587, 1km (¹/₃ mile) away

Accessibility: easy, level walk, cycle ride or pram push from car park

Times: daily; April to July are the best months to watch young birds

Contact: RSPB Regional Office (01392 432691), warden (01752
  341377, www.plymperegrines.co.uk)

Weather: avoid rain and strong winds (when the birds will not fly)

Peregrines are the fastest birds in the world. A nesting pair can be seen in amazing detail through powerful telescopes from Cann Viaduct. A pair of ravens nest nearby and both species can be watched easily throughout the breeding season. Volunteer guides are on hand to tell you more. Having your own binoculars is an advantage.

Picking wild fruit and nuts

Most children love blackberries, especially with ice cream. Old clothes and a bowl or bucket are all you need to pick blackberries, which thrive in hedges around the moorland edge. The earliest fruit are edible in late August, but September is the main month to pick them.

Whortleberries (also known as bilberries) ripen in late summer on the high moor. They have a sharp, unique taste, but picking them is slow work. You have to get down low to find the tiny, purple blue berries, which are delicious in a pie or with cream.

Hazelnuts ripen in September and October, and are ripe when the kernels are just brown all over. Hazels are abundant in the lanes around Dartmoor and so are squirrels, so be sure to get some nuts before these fascinating pests have the lot!

In short, nothing tastes better than wild fruit and nuts. Collecting them is plenty of fun, but please be careful not to trespass and not to damage hedges or trample vegetation when picking.

Blackberries, whortleberries and hazelnuts are wholesome and nutritious, but be sure you (and especially the kids) know what you are picking and don't eat too many at once. Some berries, yew for example, look attractive but should *never* be eaten. Unless you're trained, I don't recommend picking mushrooms and fungi, because some are very poisonous indeed. However, DWT and DNPA organise fungus forages in the autumn, which are interesting and quite safe – the range of flavours in our edible fungi is extraordinary.

Viewpoints

Dartmoor's viewpoints are superb, but choose a clear day. Map and compass add greatly to the interest – kids love finding things and learn a lot about map reading in the process. A few of the best and most accessible viewpoints are listed below. They offer a range of views in all directions. Several have additional points of interest.

Brent Tor, SX471804, between Tavistock and Lydford, is crowned with a small church.

Buckland Beacon, SX735732, near Buckland-in-the-Moor. The Ten Commandments were carved on a stone here in 1928.

Combestone Tor, SX670718, 2 km (1¹/₄ miles) E of Hexworthy.

Hameldown Tor, SX704806, overlooks the Bronze Age settlement of Grimspound with its 24 hut circles.

Haytor Rocks, SX757771. 750 m (800 yards) to the N is the granite tramway (1820); the stone rails are well preserved. Horse-drawn wagons took stone from nearby quarries to Teigngrace – a descent of 400 m (1300 ft) in 13.6 km (8¹/₂ miles).

Hound Tor, SX743790. Associated with local legend (page 7).

Playparks

Locations: most towns and several villages, including Bovey Tracey, Moretonhampstead, Sourton (the Highwayman Inn), Ilsington, Lustleigh, Chagford, Tavistock

We're talking about the perennially popular swings, climbing frames, see-saws, roundabouts, etc where children let off steam, build up an appetite and give their long-suffering parents a wee rest. Some, such as the playpark in Lustleigh's Orchard, the recreation ground at Chagford and Bovey Tracey's Marsh Mill Park, are in especially attractive places. Thankfully, most playparks are fenced off from dogs.

Stover Park

Cost: entry is free, but the car park has modest charges
Location: 4 km (2¹/₂ miles) S of Bovey Tracey on the A382
Accessibility: excellent, suitable for buggies and wheelchairs
Times: the park itself is always open, the visitor centre opens 10-4 in summer and at winter weekends and half terms
Contact: 01626 835236 (www.devon.gov.uk/stover_country_park)
Weather: the visitor centre is an indoor alternative
Optional: binoculars for birdwatching

Noted for its birds, Stover Park contains 114 acres of woodland, heathland, grassland, lake and marsh, with well defined paths for buggies. Just outside the Dartmoor boundary, Stover offers a pleasing contrast of scenery and is especially good when fog and rain have closed in on the high ground and the kids still want to be outdoors.

The visitor centre is designed for children (using recycled materials where possible), with interesting and attractive displays on animals, birds and plants. Kids love the giant jigsaws, the touch and feel games, the fish tank and driving the CCTV camera for close up views of birds and bugs. Outdoors again are display boards and an aerial walkway that gives remarkably close views of birds in the tree canopy. Stover is the venue for several Wildlife Watch events (page 18) and RSPB bird-watching parties. Teachers and youth leaders can contact the ranger.

Museums

Dartmoor has several museums, all offering an interesting solution to the inevitable problem of what to do with the kids on a wet day. Check out www.devonmuseums.net. This is only a selection.

High Moorland Visitor Centre, Princetown

Cost: free
Location: in the centre of the town
Parking: public car park adjacent
Accessibility: ground floor
Times: daily except Christmas and one week in March
Weather: excellent all-weather option
Contact: 01822 890414

There's enough here to occupy you and the kids for many hours, even a whole day. It is an excellent introduction to Dartmoor's landscape, wildlife, cultural heritage and history from Neolithic times to the present and is far from stuffy. The brass rubbings are designed for children. My kids also liked the legend tableaux, complete with scary photos. Try on the witches masks and look at yourself in the mirror.

An excellent 60 minute film depicts moorland life; it is largely based on interviews with local people and shows farming scenes, the annual pony drift (when ponies are rounded up from the moor and taken to market), the pony sales and Widecombe Fair. There are also oral history CDs, mainly in broad Devon speech, videos showing military training and a Country Code video which is outrageously funny.

Touch-screen computers allow visitors of most ages to explore the moor's geology and evolution, and one of them accesses the National Park's website, a real mine of information.

Museum of Dartmoor Life, Okehampton

Cost: entrance fee
Location: in the middle of town, next to the White Hart Hotel
Parking: public car parks in town
Accessibility: disabled access
Times: Easter to October Monday-Saturday; Sundays in high season
Contact: 01837 52295 (www.museumofdartmoorlife.eclipse.co.uk
   or dartmoormuseum@eclipse.co.uk)

The museum offers a good introduction to local history, especially the lives of Dartmoor's working people. Housed in a 19th century mill, it has a working waterwheel which came from what is now Roadford Reservoir. Refurbished, the museum has interactive exhibits of a Bronze Age hut and how to strike a Roman coin.

Bovey Heritage Centre, Bovey Tracey

Cost: free, donations welcome
Location: signed from Station Road
Parking: free car park
Accessibility: ground floor, level, disabled access
Times: Easter to end October: weekdays 10-12 and 2-4;
   Saturdays 10-12
Contact: 01626 834331

The beautiful railway from Newton Abbot to Moretonhampstead closed in 1959, but Bovey's characteristic station house (1866) is now restored and has an interesting local history collection. This includes railway photographs and memorabilia and a scale model of the station as it was in the 1950s. Other local collections include geological specimens, ceramics and items from Bovey School – ring the school bell and tell the time with the school's old 24 hour clock. Some 2 km (1¼ miles) of the former railway track is open, to cyclists and walkers only, from Bovey through wooded Parke Estate to Wilford Bridge. A delightful riverbank path leads back to Bovey.

Dartmoor Prison Heritage Centre, Princetown

Cost: entrance fee
Location: almost opposite the main prison gate
Parking: it has its own car park
Times: generally open all week, but phone to confirm times

A demonstration of the tilt hammer at Finch Foundry

Contact: 01822 892130 (www.dartmoor-prison.co.uk)

'Dartmoor' immediately suggests 'prison' to many people. The Heritage Centre, housed in the old prison stables, is one of the most popular in the area. Exhibits include crafts made by prisoners, many for sale. There is period machinery from the prison farms, uniforms and insignia, plus a gruesome collection of manacles, leg irons and flogging equipment.

The National Trust

If you think the National Trust is just for old fogies you're wrong. The Trust has become a very child aware and child friendly organisation, with a varied programme of special events and historical re-enactments, many designed primarily for children. Quizzes for kids are standard at most National Trust properties.

For general enquiries go to www.nationaltrust.org.uk, or phone 01392 881691 to check exact opening times, which vary from year to year. As well as protecting much of the landscape, the National Trust has several interesting properties in and around Dartmoor. Brief details are given below.

Finch Foundry, Sticklepath, Okehampton

(01837 840046)

Cost: entrance fee

Open: March to end October

This fascinating water-powered forge has three waterwheels and is still in working order. There are regular demonstrations.

Castle Drogo, Drewsteignton, Moretonhampstead

(01647 433306)

Cost: entrance fee to castle and/or grounds

Open: March to early November, gardens all year

England's most recently built castle, Drogo, towers over the spectacular Teign Gorge (there's a superb walk from the house including the gorge and riverbank) and has an attractive garden, as well as a lively events programme with much to interest children.

Lydford Gorge

(01822 822000)

Cost: entrance fee

Open: Gorge, March to October; waterfall only, November to March

The spectacular gorge and waterfall make a fascinating 5 km (3 mile) walk, suitable for fully mobile and well-shod children.

Saltram, Plympton

(01752 333500)

Cost: entrance fee to house and/or garden

Open: house March to end October; garden only, most of the winter

Saltram offers a large park and a garden for children to besport themselves. The house has a Tudor core, but is mainly Georgian.

Buckland Abbey, Buckland Monachorum, Yelverton

(01822 853607)

Cost: entrance fee to abbey and/or grounds

Open: February to December; limited opening in winter

This 700-year-old building is closely associated with Elizabethan seafarers Drake and Grenville, and has special exhibitions about them. There is a huge tithe barn and an Elizabethan garden, plus trails through the woods. Again, there is a strong events programme.

English Heritage sites

Cost: free (except Okehampton Castle)
Contact: 0117 975 0700 (www.english-heritage.org.uk)
Weather: all are outdoor sites; an Ordnance Survey map is needed to
  locate some of them

Dartmoor is very rich in prehistoric sites. Indeed, it is one of the best
preserved archaeological landscapes in Britain. The most remarkable
sites are cared for by English Heritage and are well worth a visit, especially if you and your kids use some imagination.

Imagine a procession at Merrivale's extraordinary stone rows, or
herding your flock into safety at Grimspound while hungry wolves
howl outside. Picture a long stretch in the dungeon at Lydford Castle,
or patrolling the battlements at Okehampton and meeting Lady
Howard's ghost... make up your own story, or paint a picture.

Okehampton Castle

01837 52844
Cost: entrance fee
Location: 1 km (1/2 mile) SW of town centre at SX583942
Parking: free car park
Accessibility: steps and steep slopes
Times: March to end September daily, 10-5 (10-6 in July and August)

Devon's largest castle is a dramatic ruin, full of interest. Kids will
enjoy the audio tour, plus picnics and walks by the river. Check for re-
enactments and special events, such as hawking and jousting.

Grimspound

Location: 7.5 km (5 miles) SW of Moretonhampstead at SX701809
Parking: roadside
Accessibility: steps and steep slopes

This late Bronze Age settlement includes the remains of 24 huts. These
give a remarkable picture of the size and design of our ancestors'
houses, with their tunnel entrances facing away from the prevailing
wind. Enclosed by a stone wall, it covers 1.6 hectares (4 acres) and
would have been an animal pound rather than a fortress.

*Opposite: active involvement at an event at English
Heritage's Okehampton Castle*

Houndtor deserted medieval village

Location: 3 km (1³/4 miles) south of Manaton at SX746788
Parking: Hound Tor car park (free)
Accessibility: steep slopes
Walk: 2.5 km (1¹/2 miles)

The settlement comprises the remains of three or four small farm-steads under legendary Hound Tor (page 7). Again, there is enough to build an accurate picture of the past. (Why not bring a sketch book and try drawing it?) First occupied during the Bronze Age, it was abandoned around the time of the Black Death in 1348.

Lydford Castle

Location: 13 km (8 miles) south of Okehampton
Parking: free car park in village
Accessibility: steep slopes

This imposing 12th century tower-keep became a courthouse and prison, notorious for harsh punishments.

> I oft have heard of Lydford law
> How in the morn they hang and draw
> And sit in judgment after.
>
> William Browne, 1644

Be sure not to miss the witty Watchmaker's Tomb in nearby Lydford Churchyard.

Spinster's Rock, one of dozens of fascinating prehistoric remains on Dartmoor, many of them likely to impress children

Merrivale prehistoric settlement

Location: 1 km (¹/₂ mile) east of Merrivale at SX554748
Parking: roadside car parks (free)
Accessibility: steep slopes
Walk: 1 km (¹/₂ mile)

Merrivale has two double rows of stones, each with a standing stone. There are also burial chambers and a stone circle, as well as the remains of huts. The moorland setting is superb.

Other historic and prehistoric sites

Lack of space forbids anything like a full list. However, the old engine house at Wheal Betsy mine at SX510613, 8 km (5 miles) north of Tavistock, deserves a special mention, as does the prehistoric burial chamber at Spinster's Rock, 3 km (2 miles) south of Whiddon Down at SX703907.

Becky Falls, particularly suitable for young children

Visitor attractions

Becky Falls
Cost: entrance fee
Suitable: for all ages, but especially small children
Location: 6km (4 miles) west of Bovey Tracey on the Manaton road
Parking: free parking for visitors
Accessibility: paths not suitable for wheelchairs, pushchair access
    limited, baby carriers recommended. Dogs welcome if on leads.
Times: late March to early November
Contact: 01647 221259
Refreshments: licenced cafeteria; picnic tables among the trees

Beautiful Becky Falls are best seen after rain, when the water crashes over tiers of boulders. Kids soon discover these are good for scrambling, and it's also a good place for a paddle. But for both scrambling and paddling, shoes with rubber soles are a must – the wet rock is slippery and notoriously hard.

Three attractive signed trails through the oak woods allow a variety

Otter cubs playing, at Dartmoor Otters, Buckfastleigh

of exploration, with nature trail competitions for the children and helpful plaques to explain what you are seeing. Spring with its wild-flowers, and Autumn with colours, are particularly special.

Kids, especially the youngest, will enjoy meeting the animals – miniature ponies, pygmy goats, various rabbits, chipmunks and guinea pigs. Some of the animals can be touched and groomed, though the owls and buzzards, of course, cannot. These are all rescued birds, many of them injured. They would not have survived in the wild and have found a welcome refuge here.

There are puppet shows twice daily and stories for small children, as well as pony rides for the young ones. All in all, an excellent day out for the family.

Buckfastleigh Butterflies and Dartmoor Otters
Cost: combined entrance fee; discount if also visiting South Devon
    Railway (page 38)
Location: Buckfastleigh Station, off the A38
Parking: large free car park
Accessibility: full disabled access, but the otters are difficult to see
    from a wheelchair

Times: late March to end October
Contact: 01634 642916 (www.ottersandbutterflies.co.uk)
Weather: the butterflies are a wet weather option

Over a dozen otters live at Buckfastleigh in a landscaped area, including a glass enclosure where you can see them swimming, diving and playing underwater. This is fascinating to watch – even dedicated naturalists would not see this in the wild, as otters are shy and nocturnal. They are particularly lively at feeding times (11.30, 2.00 and 4.30). Most entertaining of all are the cubs, which are usually born around Easter and can be viewed with their mother in a glass fronted holt. Apart from the entertainment, this is also an otter sanctuary.

The Butterfly Farm houses butterflies from around the world: the tropical species are much larger and more spectacular than our native butterflies. Children can watch the various stages of the life cycle in a special area where the butterflies emerge from their chrysalis, dry their wings and make their first flight.

The Butterfly Farm is a very attractive landscaped area in itself, and also houses birds, fish, frogs, lizards, terrapins and ants.

Canonteign Falls

Cost: entrance fee
Location: in the Teign valley, signed off the B3193, about 5 km
    (3 miles) north of the A38 Chudleigh junction
Parking: free car park
Accessibility: steep footpaths, slippery after rain so suitable footwear
    needed. Baby carriers recommended. Chauffered golf buggy to
    Clampitt Falls. Disabled toilet. Dogs welcome if on leads.
Times: open all year, March-November 10-6, otherwise 10 to dusk
Contact: 01647 252434 www.canonteignfalls.com
Refreshments: tea rooms offering light lunches; picnic areas

Canonoteign claims to be England's highest waterfall, with a vertical drop of 67 m (220 ft). The attractive combination of waterfalls, cascades, lakes and massive rock formations look most spectacular after heavy rain. East-facing, the falls themselves are best seen in the morning, but there is enough to see and do at Canonteign for a full day out.

Children are well catered for with brass rubbing, play areas, trampolines and a junior commando course. Donkeys and domestic animals live in the adjacent paddock. There is scope for pond dipping

Cardew Teapottery

and fly-fishing on the lake, but you'll need your own gear.

Take the children exploring on the wilderness walks, wetland nature reserve and nature trails. There are quizzes to go with these: no doubt your kids will expect you to complete them! The site has a rich variety of wildlife and plants – wild flowers in Spring and fungi in Autumn. The new owners are working closely with Devon Wildlife Trust to develop Canonteign as an educational resource.

There is a short level walk around the lakes and wetland areas, but the beautiful walk to the top of Lady Exmouth's Falls entails steps and steep paths – compensated for by superb views.

Cardew Teapottery
Cost: free admission, but charges for painting and glazing
Location: southern outskirts Bovey Tracey on A382 by roundabout
Parking: large free car park
Accessibility: ground floor, level, disabled access
Times: 10-5.30 daily throughout year
Contact: 01626 832172 (www.thecardewteapottery)
Weather: good wet weather activity, and ten acres outside to play in

Opposite: Canonteign Falls

Refreshments: restaurant offering home-cooked food

Cardew Teapottery offers children the chance to decorate ceramics and keep their own creations. All the materials are supplied and staff are on hand to advise. There are three options.

Paint and Go appeals to small children as items are ready almost immediately. Choose an item to paint from a large array of pottery moulds, including Disney characters. Paint and Glaze may appeal more to older children. It offers a variety of vases, jugs, mugs, teapots and plates, but this means leaving your decorated ceramic for the pottery to glaze and fire. Either call back or ask Cardew to post your item.

If you want the satisfaction of seeing the whole process through, the new ceramics studio enables you to cast, fettle, fire, decorate and glaze. This is advertised as 'Potty Training', but actually offers hours of interest for those well beyond the nappy stage.

Cardew also offer a free tour of the working pottery and regular demonstrations of raku firing. The shop has a range of unusual crafts, including some very original ceramics.

Dartmoor Railway

Location: Okehampton Station – follow 'Historic Station' signs

Parking: free at Okehampton station

Accessibility: wheelchair access through Okehampton station and at Meldon visitor centre; trains and Meldon buffet have partial wheelchair access

Times: trains on Saturdays and Sundays, plus certain other days. There are trains to and from Crediton and Exeter on summer Sundays only. Okehampton station shop (specialising in model railways), buffet and cycle hire are open 10-5 daily, the Meldon buffet and visitor centre 11-5 Saturdays and Sundays only

Contact: 01837 55667 (www.dartmoorrailway.co.uk)

Linked to walks, including a splendid 5 km (3 mile) circuit of Meldon Reservoir and the Granite Way Cycle route to Lydford (page 10), the Dartmoor Railway provides a lot of scope for energetic kids.

At present, vintage diesel locomotives do the work, but there are plans to re-introduce steam in the near future. From Okehampton, where the station has been restored in period Southern Railway style, the railway operates on part of the line that continued into Cornwall

Okehampton Station, headquarters of the Dartmoor Railway

in pre-Beeching days. You can still travel the line as far as Meldon and enjoy great views of Okehampton Castle (page 26) on the way.

At Meldon Quarry Station the visitor centre gives a history of the quarry and nearby Meldon Viaduct, illustrated with photographs. Meldon Viaduct remains a triumph of Victorian engineering which looks equally impressive from the cycleway above and the footpath below. It was built in 1874 to cross the West Okement. Impress your kids with the facts: six Warren girders, supported by lattice piers (the tallest is 36 m/120 ft) carry a span of 162 m/540 ft.

As well as running west to Meldon, the *Dartmoor Pony* trains also run east to Sampford Courtenay, where the station was reopened as recently as 2004. From here it is a 2.5 km (1 1/2 mile) cycle ride or walk to handsome Sampford Courtenay village. The church has a special exhibition on the 1549 Prayer Book Rebellion.

If you want to leave your car behind on summer Sundays you could go as far afield as Exeter and Plymouth from Okehampton station, or tour Dartmoor with Sunday Rover tickets. These are valid on buses and some mainline trains and offer remarkable value for money.

House of Marbles, Bovey Tracey

Cost: free – though your kids will probably inveigle you into buying some souvenir marbles; there is a superb variety of these and other goods for sale

Suitable for: all ages, but very young children need supervision as some items are fragile

Location: Pottery Road, southern outskirts of Bovey Tracey on A382

Parking: large free car park

Accessibility: ground floor level, upper floor accessible only by stairs

Times: 9-5, 7 days per week, all year bar Christmas, early January and Easter

Glassblowing displays: weekdays from Easter to end September 9-4.30 and Sundays 10-3

Refreshments: café/licensed restaurant

Contact: 01626 835358 (www.houseofmarbles.com)

Glassblowing is the highlight of a visit to the House of Marbles. Hot, coloured glass is blown by using hollow tubes and shaped with hand tools.

The House of Marbles provides much else to see – and do. You can spend hours working the fascinating Heath Robinson-like marble runs. The marbles dash around by chutes, spirals and stairs. Great! Upstairs is an even larger marble run and a snoring bear. Children paint a poster of the bear and win a teddy bear key ring. There are also stacks of children's games for sale, including classics such as spillikins, marbles, croquet, boules and wooden trains. Play a game of bagatelle or outdoor marbles by the café. This has a terrific collection of period photographs.

The House of Marbles was Bovey Tracey's industrial pottery until 1956. Pottery was the town's leading industry and the pottery had its own railway siding. Next to the café are three muffle kilns. Take the time to look inside and see how they worked.

There is also a fascinating pottery museum, with ceramics and artifacts going back to the 18th century and models of Bovey's earlier potteries. The marble museum has a good collection of historic children's toys, plus marbles of all types, some beautiful, some old and all attractive. It also shows how marbles are made and has a marble making machine.

Miniature Pony Centre

Miniature Pony Centre

Cost: entrance fee (free for children under 3); season tickets
Suitable for: younger children
Location: on B3212, 4.5 km (3 miles) west of Moretonhampstead
Parking: ample and free
Accessibility: mainly level, some slopes, disabled facilities
Times: March-October, 7 days per week, 10.30-4.30 (10-5 July and
  August)
Ideal time: spring or early summer, when the ponies foal
Contact: 01647 432400 (www.miniatureponycentre.com)
Weather: many indoor activities, so not weather dependent
Refreshments: café and licensed restaurant, lakeside picnic area

The centre's greatest strength lies in introducing young children to
safe and direct or close contact with animals – over 150, including
ponies, horses, donkeys, rabbits, guinea pigs, goats, ducks, chipmunks,
chinchillas, gerbils, mice and lambs. All the animals, including the
charmingly pint-sized ponies, are friendly, cuddly and approachable.

Every day there is a programme of fun activities, ranging from feeding the animals and birds to grooming and riding the ponies. There is also an outdoor playground, trampolines, an indoor assault course and (for the tinies) a soft indoor play centre. Altogether, this adds up to a delightful and varied day out in a very safe environment, specifically designed for children.

River Dart Adventures
Cost: Dare Devils, charge per activity; day fee for activity sessions
Mainly suitable for older children – check age and weight
    restrictions before going
Location: 2.5 km (1½ miles) from Ashburton, on the Dartmeet
    road, signed from A38
Times: Dare Devils, May half-term and summer school holidays
Contact: 01364 652511 (www.riverdart.co.uk)

River Dart Adventures (formerly the River Dart Country Park) is a huge site, packed with adventure playgrounds, play lakes and scenic woodland walks. 'Dare Devils' is a range of well-equipped activities, including a zip wire, a climbing wall, high ropes for climbing and canoeing on the lake. Day activity sessions include canoeing, caving, climbing and abseiling and are led by qualified instructors.

South Devon Railway
Cost: fares – can be combined with Buckfastleigh Butterflies and
    Dartmoor Otters for reduced admission fees
Location: Buckfastleigh Station, off the A38
Parking: large free car park
Accessibility: full disabled access from Buckfastleigh Station
Times: late March to October, and a limited winter service
Refreshments: restaurant; picnic tables

Steam enthusiasts and 'Thomas' fans will be delighted with the SDR. It follows the beautiful Dart valley from Buckfastleigh on the edge of Dartmoor to Totnes, offering the best views by far of this part of Dartmoor's chief river.

Buckfastleigh Station is packed with interest, including five steam locomotives and four diesels. The carriages are pre-1948 GWR stock, restored to prime condition. From the viewing gallery, you can watch both locos and rolling stock being restored.

On the South Devon Railway at Buckfastleigh Station

Everything works, including the signal box – watch the points move! The driver will be happy to show kids his cab while the train is waiting in the station. The railway museum includes Britain's oldest surviving broad gauge loco (1868); there are model railways, a gift and bookshop, a children's play area, riverside walks and picnic tables.

Down the line, the stations at Staverton and Totnes have been restored just as country stations used to be. Staverton is a pleasant place to wander, Totnes is a lovely historic town with a castle.

Some other useful Bossiney titles

About Dartmoor
Ancient Dartmoor
Medieval Dartmoor
The making of modern Dartmoor
Ponies on Dartmoor
Really short walks – North Dartmoor (3-5 km)
Really short walks – South Dartmoor (3-5 km)
Shortish walks on Dartmoor (5-8 km

Just some of the places referred to in this book

40